Praise for
ID REQUIRED by Dr. Joshua Fowler

As a believer we are known in Hell. Now the question remains Do we know who we are? In our Bible there are over 300 people mentioned but only about 20% fulfilled their God given destiny. The Lord desires to move each of us into our predestine purpose. In ID Required Joshua Fowler will reveal how you can discover and fulfill what God has called you as an individual to do. It is a must read for us all!

Terry Nance
Focus on the Harvest Ministries, Springdale, Arkansas
Author of: *God's Armor Bearer 1,2 & 3*
www.godsarmorbearer.com

We are living in a time where ID is vital. Since 9/11 there is a greater desire to identify those that are with us and those that are against us. In addition, we have seen the problem of absentee fathers, they have left their children without an identity and that has caused many problems in our society. Whether we want to know who is with us or who we are ID is Required! This book will place those tools at your fingertips. Also, make sure you read the chapter "How to Prevent ID Theft" it will save you much heartache and distress. My friend, Apostle Joshua Fowler has written a book filled gems and anyone who gets this book will the richer for it.

Apostle Jose G. Rodriguez
Embassy Church, San Antonio, TX
www.myembassy.com

Dr. Fowler has touched the heart of the matter for the believer who is seeking to live life as God intended when he tells us that our identity in Christ releases our destiny. Apostle Paul addresses this truth in Colossians 3:1-2, "when Christ who is our life is revealed, we also will be revealed with Him in glory". Finding out who we are is the key that unlocks every door to our legacy. Thanks for explaining this truth in such a profound manner in ID Required.

Dr. John Polis
Revival Fellowship International, Fairmont, WV
www.lifeofvictoryeveryday.net

My Friend Dr. Joshua Fowler has gone into uncharted waters. He has written a book that has been long over do. ID Required will help the Body of Christ to recognize the DNA of the Household of God. This book will help others to walk in their Identity and Destiny. This is a book for all to read. Remember, there is no business, like Kingdom Business!

Dr. Orlando Barela
Household of Faith Family Church, Orange, CA
www.householdoffaith.org

With so many people questioning who they are and why they are here, I.D. Required is right on time. Apostle Fowler has once again uncovered the enemy and his strategy. Satan knows if he can steal your identity he can get your goods. Although this battle is as old as Adam and Eve in the garden it is still one of Satan's most powerful weapons. Through this book the Holy Spirit will equip you for the battle and give you weapons you need to win it! You will be able to take back from the enemy everything he has taken from you *and* all he has in his barns as well! This book is a must read for every one.

Dr. Dan White, Sr.
Apostle, Global Impact Ministries, Jacksonville, FL
www.gimintl.com

My friend, Dr. Joshua Fowler draws attention to one of the most crucial areas of our existence – identity. Instinctively, from our core, we ask these questions. "Who am I?" "Why am I here?" "What was I created to be?" Upon discovery, we embrace that which resonates within us answering these foundational areas of our being. We then go from existence to engaging with eternal purpose and design.

During our annual conference this year in a message entitled, "Name Determines Nature", I revealed our ministry's new name. As soon as we responded to the Lord's direction, our identity began taking shape in front of us. Our mission has now begun taking direction in ways unimaginable. We're embracing it and running with passion! This book stirs my heart. Out of my own life, I can attest to the validity and urgency of Joshua's message ID REQUIRED. For this purpose he was created – to lead God's people into their Promised Land. Step up and take your place in your destiny. Request and embrace your ID. It's your inheritance! Let's possess!

Bret Wade, Apostle
Realm Ministries, Huntsville, Alabama USA
www.realmministries.com

"God is raising up new voices in the body of Christ today and Apostle Joshua Fowler is one of them. He has captured divine revelation from the heart and mind of God. This book *ID Required* is a reminder that we are qualified for greatness. This is must reading for anyone who desires to go to new levels in Christ. Thank you Apostle Fowler for sharing your insight".

Apostle J.R Gonzalez
Senior Pastor of Christian Worship Center in L.A.
www.cwcla.org

In an age where Identity Theft has become a real issue, my good friend Dr. Joshua Fowler has touched a nerve with some timely revelation on our Identity in Christ.

As you delve into the pages of this book you will see the need to be identified with Christ and the awesome benefits that are realized as you do. If you are reading this book but have lost your identity in Christ it will assist you in recovering it.

ID Required will encourage you; it will embolden your faith and give you the confidence to be all that you can be in Christ Jesus.

Read, enjoy and then go forth and BE!

Dr. Michael Scantlebury, Apostle & Sr. Elder
Dominion-Life International Ministries, Vancouver B.C.
Author of: Five Pillars of the Apostolic and others

ID REQUIRED

ID REQUIRED

DR. JOSHUA FOWLER

Printed in the United States of America

Publishing services by Legacy Press, Florida. The views expressed or implied in this work do not necessarily reflect those of Legacy Press.

ISBN: 978-1-58930-201-3

To the closest friend I have on the planet, my soul mate, my lover, my confidant, my prayer partner, the love of my life, my wife, Deborah Ashley. You truly are my help meet! You help me meet the vision for our lives! Baby, You complete me!

ACKNOWLEDGEMENTS

First and foremost I want to thank the one who helped me to discover my true identity - My Lord and Savior, my best friend - Jesus Christ!

To my dad and mom - thanks for always being there! It's an awesome thing to know that my parents believe in me enough to be a part of the Legacy Life Ministry Team! I love you.

To the one to whom I've dedicated this book, my wife, Deborah Ashley Fowler. Our Twin Daughters, Destiny and Zoë - thanks for being patient with Daddy while I worked on this book. You two rock! I love you both and I'm so proud of you! My son, Hunter - I love you to the moon and back and again and again.

To the Legacy Life Church Family - it truly is an honor to serve as your apostle. Most of what is within these pages came from the demand you place on a weekly basis on the grace God has placed on my life! Keep drawing, together we will equip and impact nations and generations for the Glory of God!

To Apostle Dan & Debbie White - Thanks for standing with my wife and I in the good and not so good times. You guys model covenant living, I'm so glad that God put you in our lives.

To all those at Selah Publishing - Garlen, Rhiannon and Christy - Thanks for helping make everything come together. I truly couldn't have done it without you!

To the following minister friends for encouraging and imparting into my life - Pastor Sunday Adelijah, Dr. Orlando & Elizabeth Barela, Bro. Buddy Bell, Apostle Tammy Chism, Dr. Jesse Duplantis, Prophet N.H Dutton, Apostle John Eckhardt, Apostle J.R. Gonzales, Apostle Eliseus & Marcia Joseph, Terry Nance, Apostle Jose G. Rodriguez, Dr. Michael & Sandra Scantlebury, Apostle Dean & Jodie Sheets, Apostle Bret Wade and Apostles Ed & Lee Watson.

Contents

INTRODUCTION

Particularly in today's society, it seems that no matter where we go or what we do, we have to have an ID for admittance. If you want to use your credit card for groceries, the clerk has to check your ID. If you want to pay for new clothes or shoes with your credit card, the associate asks for your ID. If you want to purchase a ticket, ride a plane, or pass through a secure checkpoint, even pick up your child from school...that ID is required!

Perhaps you feel like you have lived a successful life "so far"! Or maybe you desire to see God do yet greater things in and through your life—something bigger than yourself, such as a new invention or a business idea, authoring books or writing music...something that accomplishes more than what most of us would consider to be a "mediocre life." How about fulfilling a God-ordained destiny and living a life that leaves a legacy?

If you desire to maximize the potential God has placed within you to impact this world in your lifetime...then read on! Keys to help you discover your God-given identity are right at your fingertips!

YOUR FULL TIME HAS COME!

Now Elizabeth's **full time** came for her to be delivered, and she brought forth a son.
LUKE 1:57 EMPHASIS MINE

D id you know that it's time for *your* "full time" to come? Have you been waiting for the "fullness of time" to come in your life? Many of us have a "baby" on the inside of our spirits, a promise from God yet to be fulfilled! I believe we will reach the fullness of time when those promises come to pass! We are about to be visited by God's "Time Twins": "suddenly" and "immediately" are about to jump into the wrestling rings of our lives and pounce on our en-

---

We are about to be visited by God's "Time Twins." "Suddenly and Immediately" are about to jump into the wrestling rings of our lives and pounce on our enemies!

---

emies! I wrote more about God's Time Twins in the prequel to this book: *ACCESS GRANTED!* I believe that God will release His Time Twins into our lives more and more as we come into our identity!

The promise God had given Elizabeth was something that she couldn't bring about on her own. She and her husband, Zacharias, were unable to have children, but in their old age, God promised to give them a son. Let's look back at this promise from the Lord.

17

> Then an angel of the Lord appeared to him, standing on the right side of the altar of incense. And when Zacharias saw him, he was troubled, and fear fell upon him. But the angel said to him, "Do not be afraid, Zacharias, for your prayer is heard; and your wife Elizabeth will bear you a son, and you shall call his name John." And you will have joy and gladness, and many will rejoice at his birth. "For he will be great in the sight of the Lord, and shall drink neither wine nor strong drink. He will also be filled with the Holy Spirit, even from his mother's womb. "And he will turn many of the children of Israel to the Lord their God. He will also go before Him in the spirit and power of Elijah, 'to turn the hearts of the fathers to the children,' and the disobedient to the wisdom of the just, to make ready a people prepared for the Lord."
>
> LUKE 1:11–17

What an amazing experience that would be! The prayers of Zacharias and Elizabeth had been heard—and answered! Zacharias was astonished.

> And Zacharias said to the angel, "How shall I know this? For I am an old man, and my wife is well advanced in years." And the angel answered and said to him, "I am Gabriel, who stands in the presence of God, and was sent to speak to you and bring you these glad tidings. But behold, you will be mute and not able to speak until the day these things take place, because you did not believe my words which will be fulfilled in their own time."
>
> LUKE 1:18-20

There may be some things that have been spoken over your life that have remained unfulfilled and have frustrated you. You may pray, *God, why has this not come to pass? Lord, why is this yet to happen? I know Your prophet said this would happen, but I haven't seen it yet!* Have you ever felt like that? What's going on? Why aren't we walking in the destinies God has for us, which He has promised?

This is especially frustrating when you've been walking in obedience to the Lord. You've been faithful. You've been consistent. You've been doing everything He's told you to do. You've been like Enoch, walking with God, waiting for the day when God brings to pass His promises. But I'm here to tell you that the day is coming when there will be a catching away—you're about to be caught up in your destiny.

You're not waiting on destiny—destiny's waiting on you. You're not waiting on God—God is waiting on you!

WHAT TIME IS IT?

The Bible tells us that we are able to understand the times and seasons of the Lord: *"the children of Issachar had understanding of the times"* (1 Chronicles 12:32).

One of our problems today is that most people don't know how to tell time God's way. In the Body of Christ, we have people who can prophesy well, but they can't discern the time of the prophecy: They don't know if it is to take place in the past, the present, or the future. But God is ready to bring His people into an understanding of times and seasons like never before.

At the dawn of each day, you should ask God, "Lord, how do You want me to tell time today? What time is it to You? Is it time to see someone healed? Is it time to see someone set free? Is it time to cast out the devil?" Wherever you go and whatever you do, you should be living your life on God's timetable.

Wherever you go and whatever you do, you should be living your life on God's timetable.

Many of us are living on our own timetables. We continue to do the same things day in and day out, limited to what we can see with our natural eyes. But we need to remember that God has stepped outside of time. God is in eternity. God is the Alpha, and He's the Omega. He was at the beginning of the race when you started it! And He's at the end of the race saying, "Come on, son. Come on, daughter. I'm here. I'm ready to receive you!" When you begin to get a picture of life from His perspective, you're catching a glimpse of what eternity is like. In one instant, everything can be revealed. In one moment, things will happen that you've waited a lifetime to see. You never know how close you are to what God has for you—so you cannot give up!

There is, however, something that precedes your destination. God is waiting for you to do something: to agree with what He said. You may think that you already agree with the Lord, but He may be waiting for your mental assent to move down so deep in your spirit that your belief and trust in Him is like fire shut up in your bones. You can't keep it quiet! You're possessed with the Spirit of the Lord, and you can't contain His destiny for you anymore. You are certain beyond a shadow of a doubt that God's promises are "yes and amen." They *will* come to pass!

There comes a point in your life when it doesn't matter what your so-called qualifications are: If you're a part of the choir, it doesn't matter. If you're part of Who's Who in American Churches, it is irrelevant. It doesn't make a difference if one preacher or another has blown his breath on you, or rubbed oil on your forehead, or even prophesied over you. If you've got the Word of God in your spirit, your destiny is assured—your time will surely arrive!

Before you reach that point, however, there's something you will have to overcome. What is preventing you from going from point A to point B? What is keeping you from your destiny? How can you step into it? How can you achieve the greatness that God has for your life?

Many of us believe it is the devil that is preventing us from living out what God wants to do in and through us. But the devil is not big enough to stop a move of God that the Lord will accomplish in the earth. God's Word says that just one of us can put a thousand to flight, and two of us can put ten thousand to flight! We serve a great God, and His power is more than able to be made manifest in our lives. There aren't enough devils in the world to stop what He wants to do.

So, what is hindering us, if it's not the devil? What is keeping us from our destinies? Let's look back to the Word of God.

> And the people waited for Zacharias, and marveled that he lingered so long in the temple. But when he came out, he could not speak to them; and they perceived that he had seen a vision in the temple, for he beckoned to them and remained speechless.
>
> Luke 1:21–22

Shut Your Mouth!

D id you catch what happened to Zacharias? He did not believe what God had said, and so he "could not speak unto them." God was trying to remove what was standing between this man and his destiny: namely, his mouth! Maybe that is a word that you need to hear today: "Shut your mouth!" Your words may be the very thing that is standing in the way of your fulfilling the promises that God has made to you.

If your mouth is standing between you and what God has for you, then you are not speaking the right thing. If you are saying anything other than what God's Word says, then you're not claiming God's promises. Before you put this book down and dismiss me as just one of those "name it and claim it" preachers, think about what I am saying.

Ask yourself: What is in your mouth? What is coming out of your mouth? Are you "foaming out of the mouth" with doubt and unbelief, or are you speaking words of faith and life regarding your destiny?

What you say is what you will get. You will have whatever you speak into existence. The enemy is fueled by words of doubt and God responds to words of faith. The power of death—and of life—is found in our tongues (Proverbs 18:21).

Many of us are hung up by the tongue. We don't even realize this is often the reason why our finances are shrinking, that's why many marriages are falling apart. We speak things that are contrary to what God actually wants to give us: "That costs too much for me to have; I'll never be able to afford that!" No, no, no! We've got to change our thinking and our speaking! Instead, we should say, "I'll be back for you!" I've heard some people say some crazy things like, "I just don't know about my old man." Some women say, "My old man, he ain't got no j-o-b." Guess what? You will have whatsoever you say. If you continually speak those kinds of words, then that is exactly what you'll get: an old man with no j-o-b. If you want an old lady, then just call your wife one long enough, and you will have what you say! I call my wife, "Baby Doll," "Pretty Woman," and "Beautiful," and you know what? She looks better and better every day! We met when we were twelve years old at youth camp, and she looks better now than she did then!

So many people do this without even thinking. We speak things over our children. We say things about different members of our families. And what we're speaking lends power to the forces of darkness that want to destroy our lives. God may need to do something drastic with some of us—just like He did with Zacharias: He might shut our mouths. If you can't agree with what the Word of God says, just shut your mouth!

Many of us spend all of our lives saying the *wrong* things and wondering why we're not coming into the *right* things. As with Zacharias, it is best to just shut your mouth. Even better, though, is to be like Mary instead of Zacharias. In the very same chapter of Luke, Mary demonstrated her faith in God's promise by responding with: *"… be it unto me according to thy word"* (verse 38).

"BE IT UNTO ME!"

When God makes a promise to you, instead of saying, "How, God?" you need to say, "Yes, Lord!" You need to be just like Mary in this passage of scripture. Why did God choose her? Because she said, "Be it unto me according to Your word," not, "How in the world is this going to happen?" Because of her faithful, obedient words, Mary received the favor of the Lord.

When God makes a promise to you, instead of saying, "How, God?" you need to say, "Yes, Lord!"

After she made this declaration of faith, the angel departed from Mary, and she journeyed into the hill country with haste. She was on her way to visit her relatives: Zacharias and his wife, Elizabeth.

> Now Mary arose in those days and went into the hill country with haste, to a city of Judah, and entered the house of Zacharias and greeted Elizabeth. And it happened, when Elizabeth heard the greeting of Mary, that the babe leaped in her womb; and Elizabeth was filled with the Holy Spirit. Then she spoke out with a loud voice and said, "Blessed are you among women, and blessed is the fruit of your womb! But why is this granted to me, that the mother of my Lord should come to me? For indeed, as soon as the voice of your greeting sounded in my ears, the babe leaped in my womb for joy. Blessed is she who believed, for there will be a fulfillment of those things which were told her from the Lord."
>
> LUKE 1:39–45

YOUR BABY IS ABOUT TO LEAP!

Think about this scenario for a moment. As soon as Jesus, within His mother's womb, entered the room, His "forerunner" leaped inside of his own mother's womb and said, "Here's the One! This is the reason I was conceived—He is here!"

Now, Elizabeth was in about her second trimester, carrying the prophet we know as John the Baptist, but as of yet, she had not felt him move inside of her. This was her first child, and she was growing older by this time, so it was very likely of great concern to her to feel her baby move. Elizabeth might have even been worried that her baby was dead. You yourself may not have felt your destiny "move" in a while. You may not have felt your baby moving. You're wondering if your destiny, that thing that God has promised you, is dead. But as soon as the Lord came into that room, the promised one, that baby, John, leapt in his mother's womb, so strongly that she knew it was of God.

DIVINE CONNECTION

When you make your divine connection, that pinnacle moment when your life gets put on course, your destiny will begin to leap inside of you, as well! What's between you and your destiny? That divine connection. When you come into contact with the people to whom you're called to minister, your destiny will begin to come alive. When Elizabeth encountered Mary, the baby leapt to life inside of her—he responded to the One to whom he was called to minister. Likewise, until you find that divine connection, the promises of God for you may feel like they are dead. Your life may feel purposeless. But when you encounter that person, that situation, that your life was meant to impact, your destiny will burst into life on the inside of you.

When you're connected with the right people, your full time will come into being.

Follow me back to God's Word:

> And Mary remained with her about three months, and returned to her house. Now Elizabeth's full time came for her to be delivered, and she brought forth a son. When her neighbors and relatives heard how the Lord had shown great mercy to her, they rejoiced with her.
>
> LUKE 1:56–58

When you're connected with the right people, your full time will come into being. Elizabeth's full time came that she would be delivered and she brought forth a son! You, too, are going to bring forth the child—the dream, the vision, the idea, the promise—that God has planted in your life. What God has said concerning your life will be brought to fruition. Even Elizabeth's neighbors and cousins heard how the Lord had showed great mercy to her, and they rejoiced with her. She was living in a community of people who were watching and were able to see how God had blessed her, and they were able to share in that amazing time.

> So it was, on the eighth day, that they came to circumcise the child; and they would have called him by the name of his father, Zacharias. His mother answered and said, "No; he shall be called John."
>
> LUKE 1:59–60

"ZACH JR." OR "JOHN"

On the eighth day, they were about to circumcise the child according to the Jewish traditions. Did you know that the number eight is the number of new beginnings? Elizabeth and Zacharias—and the entire world—were about to have a new beginning because of what God had done. When the ceremony was about to begin, they called the baby Zacharias, or "Zach Jr.," because that was his father's name and this was the firstborn son. But his mother answered quickly and said, "NO!" Instead, she declared that the baby boy would be called John.

At that time, family names meant more, much more, than they mean to us today. In our culture, occasionally a son will be named after his father, but back at that time, it was even more important to carry the family name into the future. That is why the people were astonished when they heard Elizabeth's pronouncement.

> They said to her, "There is no one among your relatives who is called by this name."
>
> LUKE 1:61

There was nobody in their family with the name of John, and the people didn't know what to think. Had the milkman come by? Why *wouldn't* they name the baby Zacharias after his father—especially after what a miracle God had done in their lives?

Remember, as we look at the next verse, that Zacharias still wasn't able to talk. He had been mute ever since he had doubted God's promise about the child that was to be born.

> So they made signs to his father—what he would have him called. And he asked for a writing tablet, and wrote, saying, "His name is John." So they all marveled. Immediately his mouth was opened and his tongue loosed, and he spoke, praising God.
> LUKE 1:62–64

HIS NAME IS JOHN

The people made signs to his father, asking what they should call the baby—even though they knew that Zacharias couldn't talk! But he asked for a writing tablet, and he wrote out his wishes: "His name is John." Notice the wording there: He didn't say his name "will be called John." He didn't say "call his name John." He said "his name *is* John." There's a difference! By saying "his name is John," Zacharias was standing in agreement with what God had settled in stone from the foundations of the earth. He was aligning himself with the promise he had been given and declaring it to be.

And look at the response of the people: *"And they marveled all."* Right then, the Bible says in verse 64, his mouth was opened *"immediately."* Are you ready to come into an "immediately"? Are you ready to release what's inside of you, waiting to burst forth? Are you ready for miracles and healing in your life? All of those things are contingent upon you coming into agreement with what God has promised you! As soon as Zacharias told the people (through writing) that "his name is John," his mouth opened up. After nine months of silence, his tongue was loosed. How did it happen? This is the key. *Proper identification.*

MISIDENTIFIED

You may be waiting right now to come into your destiny, but in order for you to make it to your destination, you have to have the right identification. ID is required! Particularly in today's society, you can't just jump on an airplane and go anywhere you want to go—even if you have a ticket. If you don't have a picture ID, you aren't getting on that plane! You can't access the money in your bank account if you don't have the right identification. You can't get into a safety-deposit box without the proper ID.

You may be waiting for your breakthrough, but you have to have the right identification first. You may have gotten the principles down, believing for access, believing for acceleration, believing for abundance, but God desires to "change your name" and give you the right ID to access all of His blessings. Man may have named you wrong. Religious systems may have called you by other names, when God has called you by *His* name, and as soon as you get out from under the bondage of a religious system and you get under the proper identification, you're going to begin to see the demonstration of what God's spoken into your life. As long as you're still under what man has said, you will be "Zack Jr.", and that is all you may ever be.

People may have misidentified you and your destiny. Other people may be trying to keep you down or discouraging you, by saying that you will never achieve anything in your life. But the most important question you can ask yourself is: What did Christ destine you to be? Some people may try to put you in a box and limit you—if you allow them to—but what God is saying to you is what really matters! Every word that proceeds out of the mouth of the Lord will come to pass! Don't allow yourself to be limited with the wrong name, with the wrong identity. There is a destiny for you—there is a reason you were put on this planet at this particular time. You have a purpose! You are not an accident! And God will help you determine your identity in Him and fulfill all the dreams He has placed within your heart.

DIVINE VISITATION RELEASES PROPER IDENTIFICATION

The Lord came to me on June 12, 1998, and He changed my identification forever. I know what it means to have to learn to spell my name all over again! I know what it means to be in a crowd of people and have to learn when my name is being spoken. I know what it means to have my wife to have to learn to call me by a new name. I know what it means to be rejected by my family because they were not in agreement with my new name. In the middle of what God was doing in my life, they rejected me, but God accepted me. Since that pinnacle moment blessings and breakthrough have continuously taken place!

I know what it means to tell my grandmother that the Lord came to me and said, "Your name shall be Joshua. Lead My people into the Promised Land." When I told my grandmother, she said, "If you were my child, I would disown you." I know what it means to have my sister block the phone and for me to not be able to call my only sibling. I know what it means for them to renounce me as if I were dead. It took three years and four days before my family was able to accept me for who I was.

"Your name shall be Joshua. Lead My people into the Promised Land."

But I also know what it means for my nature to begin to change. People who have been around this ministry and have known me from the beginning noticed a dramatic change in my personality. God began to change my nature when He changed my name. The Lord lifted me up into that heavenly place, that place of glory, and it felt like liquid gold was running up beneath my neck. Jesus stood at my feet, and out of His mouth proceeded words like waterfalls. They poured into my spirit man, and He gave me my new name, Joshua, and my new calling: to help lead His people to their Promised Land.

Now I am not talking about some wacky following. I am talking about the grace of God released upon me to encourage and lead both believers in Christ and potential believers in Christ to pursue God's purpose for their life passionately! At that time, I had no idea what the fullness of those words would mean. Even today, every day I'm continually learning and God is bringing His promises to pass. The picture is becoming clearer—and I know that even as God helped me find my proper ID, He can use me to help properly ID other people who have been misidentified, and help them enter their own Promised Land.

I'm happy to report that on Father's Day, three years and four days after my name was changed by the Lord, my dad came to minister at Legacy Life. The Lord had kept him awake all night because my dad had said, "The only way I'm ever going to call him Joshua is if God Himself visits me and tells me to do that." So the Lord Himself came down and kept Dad up all night long—and told him that my name was Joshua. The Lord asked, "Why don't you agree, as his natural father on the earth, with what I have said about him from the heavens? I'm his heavenly Father, so you should agree with what I've said. His name is Joshua!"

During the middle of the service that night as my dad ministered, he began to weep before the Lord. He said from that night forward, he would call me Joshua. This truly was a miracle because my dad had said he would never accept the name change. That night was a turning point in our relationship.

I watched as there began to be a change in my extended family. My parents relocated to base their ministry out of Legacy Life. I walked through years of pain, not feeling welcome at home for Christmas or Thanksgiving, but I was determined to walk with the identification that God had given me instead of what man had given me. And now God has restored my family, and I give God praise for it. I'm closer now to my dad than I've ever been in my life.

YOUR INHERITANCE IS IN YOUR IDENTITY

Then Abram fell on his face, and God talked with him, saying: "As for Me, behold, My covenant is with you, and you shall be a father of many nation**s. No longer shall your name be called Abram, but your name shall be Abraham; for I have made you a father of many nations.** I will make you exceedingly fruitful; and I will make nations of you, and kings shall come from you. And I will establish My covenant between Me and you and your descendants after you in their generations, for an everlasting covenant, to be God to you and your descendants after you."

GENESIS 17: 3–7, EMPHASIS MINE

Then God said to Abraham, "As for Sarai your wife, **you shall not call her name Sarai, but Sarah shall be her name.** And I will bless her and also give you a son by her; then I will bless her, **and she shall be a mother of nations;** kings of people shall be from her."

GENESIS 17:15–16 EMPHASIS MINE

IDENTITY = CAPACITY = DESTINY

Abraham could have never been the father of nations with the name "Abram." Sarah could have never been a mother of nations with the name "Sarai." Their identity limited their destiny. Their identity did not have the capacity to fulfill their destiny. Abraham and Sarah would have never received their inheritance if they had never embraced their ID! Think about it: The joy and blessing of the birth of their son Isaac, the Promised Land, the twelve tribes, and the nation of Israel would never have existed had these two members of the Hall of Faith refused to allow their identities to be changed!

Their identity did not have the capacity to fulfill their destiny. Abraham and Sarah would have never received their inheritance if they had never embraced their ID!

For if the inheritance [is] of the law, [it] is no longer of promise; but God gave [it] to Abraham by promise.
GALATIANS 3:18

And if you [are] Christ's, then you are Abraham's seed, and heirs according to the promise.
GALATIANS 3:29

36

"Remember Abraham, Isaac, and Israel, Your servants, to whom You swore by Your own self, and said to them, 'I will multiply your descendants as the stars of heaven; and all this land that I have spoken of I give to your descendants, and they shall inherit [it] forever!'"

ExODUS 32:13

"Look to Abraham your father, and to Sarah [who] bore you; for I called him alone, and blessed him and increased him."

ISAIAH 51:2

And the Scripture was fulfilled which says, "Abraham believed God, and it was accounted to him for righteousness." And he was called the friend of God.

JAMES 2:23

Our inheritance is wrapped up in our true identity.

Because Abraham and Sarah received their ID, you and I have been grafted into the vine through Christ, and we are now heirs according to the promise! We have access to our inheritance because they received their ID. Now all we have to do is receive our ID and walk in it! As heirs of the promise, we are called to possess the land. We are anointed to multiply, increase, and inherit! We are the friends of God! Our inheritance is wrapped up in our true identity.

YOUR NAME IS A CONTAINER

The name God gives you is a container that carries His expression of your nature to other people. It speaks of your nature, calling, destiny, and your purpose in life. When you have the right name—the proper identity—that ID will serve as a spiritual container and will help carry the fruit of your life to the right destination. The wrong container, or ID, will restrict and limit the productivity of your life. The right container, or ID, will maximize your productivity!

EVEN CHRIST HAD TO BE IDENTIFIED!

When He had been baptized, Jesus came up immediately from the water; and behold, the heavens were opened to Him, and He saw the Spirit of God descending like a dove and alighting upon Him. And suddenly a voice came from heaven, saying, **"This is My beloved Son, in whom I am well pleased."**
MATTHEW 3:16–17, EMPHASIS MINE

Christ's obedience to be baptized opened the way to His being identified by His Father. Identification as the Son of God gave Christ access to His inheritance, to His ability to administer miracles, healings, and so much more!

AND THAT'S NOT ALL!

It's also very important to realize that warfare often accompanies identification. I would like to say that everything is going to be wonderful once you've received your ID; however, this is not the case. Just look at the life of Christ and you will quickly begin to understand that once He received His ID, it wasn't all easy. Christ encountered warfare immediately after He was identified as the Son of God. You may ask, why? I'm so glad you asked! You see, all of hell shudders in fear at the very thought of a believer receiving his or her ID. This is the reason that many people experience such resistance from the enemy for so long. The devil would like to keep us deceived so that we will never understand who we truly are in Christ. Once we find our ID, he turns up the heat to try to get us to back down and go back to our comfort zones, where there is less warfare and struggles.

All of hell shudders in fear at the very thought of a believer receiving his or her ID.

Then Jesus was led up by the Spirit into the wilderness to be **tempted by the devil.** And when He had fasted forty days and forty nights, afterward He was hungry. Now when the tempter came to Him, he said, **"If You are the Son of God,** command that these stones become bread." But He answered and said, "It is written, 'Man shall not live by bread alone, but by every word that proceeds from the mouth of God.'" Then the devil took Him up into the holy city, set Him on the pinnacle of the Temple, and said to Him, **"If You are the Son of God**, throw Yourself down. For it is written: 'He shall give His angels charge over you,' and, 'In their

---

Christ realized something so profound and yet so simple: True authority was found within His identity!

---

hands they shall bear you up, lest you dash your foot against a stone.'" Jesus said to him, "It is written again, 'You shall not tempt the LORD your God.'" Again, the devil took Him up on an exceedingly high mountain, and showed Him all the kingdoms of the world and their glory. And he said to Him, **"All these things I will give You, if You will fall down and worship me."** Then Jesus said to him, "Away with you, Satan! For it is written, 'You shall worship the LORD your God, and Him only you shall serve.'" Then the devil left Him, and behold, angels came and ministered to Him.

MATTHEW 4:1–11, EMPHASIS MINE

The first thing the enemy did after Christ received His ID as the Son of God was to question it! Notice that in verse 3, the tempter said, "If You are the Son of God...." The very thing that the Father told Christ He was, is the very thing the enemy tried to steal—His ID! The first two times the tempter questioned His identity with the phrase, "If You are the Son of God...." The next time the enemy turned up the heat and presented an offer. The only problem was, Christ knew who He was and that He already possessed everything the tempter was offering. You see, Christ realized something so profound and yet so simple: True authority was found within His identity! Just as Christ's authority came from His ID, so will yours.

HEAVEN'S WITNESS
PROTECTION PROGRAM

Are you experiencing warfare? That's okay! You are protected. God's got the best coverage plan! If you will allow Him to change your ID, He will put you in Heaven's Witness Protection Program. Look at the success rate of Heaven's Witness Protection Plan: Israel found safety from Esau, and Peter wasn't sifted as wheat. Instead, Israel became a nation, and Peter gathered souls like wheat by the thousands!

Beloved, this is why you must fight for your ID. Don't let anything sway you. Don't allow any circumstance, situation, trial, accusation, discouraging word, disappointment, or ANYTHING else to steal your ID! If you will hold on and fight for it, you will flow in the power and demonstration of the Holy Spirit!

> Then Jesus returned in the power of the Spirit
> to Galilee, and news of Him went out through
> all the surrounding region.
> LUKE 4:14

AN ALTERNATE ROUTE?

Often, many people would rather look for an alternate route or a shortcut. Just ask the seven sons of Sceva if it's wise to take a shortcut or an alternate route. They would tell you what happens to those who go out without the ID that's required.

> Then some of the itinerant Jewish exorcists took it upon themselves to call the name of the Lord Jesus over those who had evil spirits, saying, "We exorcise you by the Jesus whom Paul preaches." Also there were seven sons of Sceva, a Jewish chief priest, who did so. And the evil spirit answered and said, "Jesus I know, and Paul I know; but who are you?" Then the man in whom the evil spirit was leaped on them, overpowered them, and prevailed against them, so that they fled out of that house naked and wounded.
> ACTS 19:13–16

The King James Version calls these itinerant exorcists "vagabonds." There are far too many "vagabonds" in the Church today! Too many people are wandering around without their IDs, looking for shortcuts or alternate routes. Like the seven sons of Sceva, these "vagabonds" will find out sooner or later that there's no way around having their ID. In the words of an American Express commercial, "Don't leave home without it!"

WHO IN HELL ARE YOU?

The demon said, "Jesus I know, and Paul I know; but who are you?" Even the enemy recognizes a true ID! This is all the more reason why we must wait until we can walk in the maturity of our identity before tackling things outside of our "weight class." Demons know and fear those who know who they are in Christ! You must know your ID and who you are in the Spirit! The enemy fights from a level of knowing who we are, so *we* had better know who we are, also. He will try to lie and deceive you so he can keep you walking beneath your level of authority. You are who God says you are, not what the enemy has lied to you about! Once you get this truth in your spirit, the enemy won't be able to stop you! You can't combat the enemy with the wrong ID; you have got to see yourself the way Christ sees you and fight from that position! Remember, true authority only comes from your identity in Christ, and this identity is found through intimacy with Christ. Paul recognized this, and that is why the demons said, "Paul I know!" Just look at the following passages of Scripture and see how Paul realized his identity in Christ:

You can't combat the enemy with the wrong ID; you have got to see yourself the way Christ sees you and fight from that position!

> For **in Him** we live and move and have our being.
>
> ACTS 17:28, EMPHASIS MINE

I have been crucified with Christ; it is no longer I who live, but **Christ lives in me;** and the life which I now live in the flesh **I live by faith in the Son of God,** who loved me and gave Himself for me.

GALATIANS 2:20, EMPHASIS MINE

To them God willed to make known what are the riches of the glory of this mystery among the Gentiles: which is **Christ in you, the hope of glory**.

COLOSSIANS 1:27, EMPHASIS MINE

PENIEL PERSISTENCE

Returning to the Old Testament, in Genesis 32, we find a man by the name of Jacob.

Then Jacob was left alone; and a Man wrestled with him until the breaking of day. Now when He saw that He did not prevail against him, He touched the socket of his hip; and the socket of Jacob's hip was out of joint as He wrestled with him.

GENESIS 32:23–25

It takes determination to live your destiny! You must persist with bulldog faith! You can never let go of what God has promised you.

Look at the next verse:

> And He said, "Let Me go, for the day breaks." But he said, "I will not let You go unless You bless me!"
>
> GENESIS 32:26

WHAT'S YOUR NAME?

Jacob had said that he was not going to let go until he was blessed. But the response that was given was, "What is your name?" This makes an important point: Your identification is directly connected to your breakthrough...to your blessing! You may have had the same kind of bulldog faith that Jacob had, hanging on until God delivers on His promise. You may be praying, "God, when am I going to see what I've been praying for?" But look at God's response to you: "What's your name? You've identified yourself spiritually with men rather than with Me. You've taken on the name of a religious system. But My ID is required for the blessings I want to give!"

I'm not talking here about natural names. I'm talking about spiritual identification. You don't have to worry about literally changing the name your parents gave you—unless that is something that God tells you to do. That's not what I'm saying here. But I am saying that you must be properly identified in your destiny. You must know who you are in Christ!

In Jacob's case, God changed his name and revealed his destiny.

> So He said to him, "What is your name?" He said, "Jacob." And He said, "Your name shall no longer be called Jacob, but Israel; for you have struggled with God and with men, and have prevailed." Then Jacob asked, saying, "Tell me Your name, I pray." And He said, "Why is it that you ask about My name?" And He blessed him there. So Jacob called the name of the place Peniel: "For I have seen God face to face, and my life is preserved."
> GENESIS 32:28–30

Do you ever wonder what Jacob was thinking in that moment? What if he *didn't* want his name to be changed? What if he was wondering, *What does this have to do with me being blessed?* At that time, Jacob was in some serious trouble. His brother, Esau, was chasing after him, ready to kill him for stealing his birthright. How in the world could a name change like this possibly help Jacob's situation? What could it possibly have to do with Jacob's destiny?

In fact, the name change was absolutely critical for Jacob to live out God's plans for his life. The name *Jacob* meant "deceiver, conniver." And all of his life, everywhere Jacob went, he lived up to that name. He had to steal everything he got. He had to fight for everything he had. He had to deceive for every blessing he had been given—because that was his nature. He had been named that, and out of that name, his very nature sprang forth.

How you are identified is of critical importance to the path your life will take.

You may have been misidentified by your family, by friends, or other people. They said you would never be able to do this, that you'd never get a real education, that you'd never make anything of yourself. Have you ever been told you would never amount to anything in your life? God wants to remove that wrong identification off of your life!

> And Esau said, "Is he not rightly named Jacob? For he has supplanted me these two times. He took away my birthright, and now look, he has taken away my blessing!" And he said, "Have you not reserved a blessing for me?"
> GENESIS 27:34

You see as long as Jacob was misidentified he was unable to fulfill his purpose in the earth. He was properly identified when his name was changed to Israel, and from that moment on, he was able to fulfill everything that God had ordained for his life!

God renamed Jacob in accordance with the destiny He had for him. His name would no longer mean "conniver" or "deceiver," but instead, "Israel"! "Israel" means "soldier of God," or "God prevailed." The Bible talks about having favor with God and men; it says that Jesus increased in wisdom, in stature, and in favor with God and with men (see Luke 2:52).

Did you know that this is God's plan for your life, too? Jacob stood strong and persisted, eventually prevailing and receiving God's favor—and that of men, as well. That's the key. He persisted. He would not let God go even to the point that he ended up walking with a limp. He held on even when his hip was out. I can only imagine the physical pain that Jacob must have endured to hold on to God's promise like that. But hold on, he did! And it was worth it in the end.

Are you a person who will prevail? Are you someone who can hold on even when it doesn't look good? Are you willing to stay connected to God even when it seems as though everybody else is going the other way? Are you tenacious about the promises of God? Are you holding on until you get what you came for?

Jacob said, "I'll not let You go until you bless me! Go ahead, and touch my other hip. I'll still hold on to You! Take my teeth out, and I'll gnaw You with my gums! I'm holding on to You!" Can you see Jacob's determination? He had the hunger. The desire. The passion. The tenacity. The persistence. Those very character traits prompted God to change his name—to Israel. An entire nation would come from him. Jacob had such persistence that God said that all the eyes of the world would forever be on this nation that came out of his loins. There would be twelve tribes that would come from his body and make up this nation—and we can see that nation even in our time today, thousands of years later.

As soon as the proper identification came, the twelve sons were called forth. Although they had not yet been born, their destinies had been birthed. One by the name of Joseph would end up saving them all—and give us yet another example of God bringing our dreams to pass. Can you see the breakthrough that comes from just one man's proper identification?

> Then Jacob asked, saying, "Tell me Your name, I pray." And He said, "Why is it that you ask about My name?" And He blessed him there. So Jacob called the name of the place Peniel: "For I have seen God **face to face**, and my life is preserved."
>
> GENESIS 32:30, EMPHASIS MINE

FACE TO FACE

Jacob had a face-to-face experience with God. God is looking for people who will stop seeking His hand...and begin to seek His face. Your identity is found in Christ! As soon as you seek His face, you will be properly identified and come into the place that God has for your life.

Reverse the Curse and Release the Blessing

Deuteronomy 33 gives us information concerning another man, Jacob's son Reuben, who received a different identity in God. This passage tells of the blessing that the twelve sons of Israel received from Moses.

> "Let Reuben live, and not die, Nor let his men be few."
>
> Deuteronomy 33:6

If you go back and look in Genesis 49, you will see that the original blessing over Reuben was very different.

> And Jacob called his sons and said, "Gather together, that I may tell you what shall befall you in the last days: Gather together and hear, you sons of Jacob, And listen to Israel your father. Reuben, you are my firstborn, My might and the beginning of my strength, the excellency of dignity and the excellency of power. Unstable as water, you shall not excel, because you went up to your father's bed; Then you defiled it—He went up to my couch."
>
> Genesis 49:1–4

The beginning of Reuben's blessing started out great: *"Thou art my firstborn, my might and the beginning of my strength, the excellency of dignity...the excellency of power...."* But then things changed, and his father proclaimed a negative identity over his son: *"You will be as unstable as water. You will not excel...."* Reuben had sinned, this is true, but at the end of his life, his father identified that this is the way it would be, not just for Reuben but also for all of his descendents!

Thank God that in Deuteronomy 33 Moses reversed what had been spoken about Reuben, and he said, *"Let Reuben live and not die and let not his men be few."* The identification that man had put on Reuben by an angry father was declared null and void! It is time for you to come into your proper identification, as well, so you can see your destiny come to pass. It is time for layers of misidentification to come off of you and for the correct mantel to be properly identified.

There is power in your true identity. You have a destiny in the Lord! You are blessed! The Word says that everything you put your hand to, it shall prosper. It says that you are more than a conqueror. It says that you can do all things through Christ who strengthens you. You shall no longer be limited, but you shall arise in your destiny and you shall possess what God has for you. You have been blessed with the power to get wealth. You have been given the spirit of increase. You have the mind of Christ. You are the head and not the tail, above only and not beneath. You shall lend and not borrow. Not many days from now, you shall come into your fullness of time and you shall give birth to the destiny that's on the inside of you!

SOME SAY!

S o how can you begin to find the identity that God has for you—the unique calling He has placed upon you? Let's take a look in the New Testament, and see how Jesus has answered this question:

> When Jesus came into the region of Caesarea Philippi, He asked His disciples, saying, "Who do men say that I, the Son of Man, am?" So they said, "Some say John the Baptist, some Elijah, and others Jeremiah or one of the prophets." He said to them, "But who do you say that I am?" Simon Peter answered and said, "You are the Christ, the Son of the living God."
> MATTHEW 16:13–16

WHO DO YOU SAY?

T he question that Jesus asked His disciples is the key: "Who do men say that I am?" There are many different answers to this question: some say John the Baptist, some say Elijah, and others Jeremiah, or one of the prophets. But then Jesus asked the most important question of all, the question that He's asking you and me today: "But who do *you* say that I am?"

We find here in Scripture the only way to find our true identity—not what man has put on us, not what we have taken upon ourselves, but the ID that is required to come into our destiny. The only way we can find that identity is when we properly identify ourselves with Christ. Our identity is in Christ. Without properly identifying Him as Lord, without properly identifying Him as the Son of the living God, neither you nor I will ever come into the fullness of our destiny.

Jesus tells us how we receive this identity in the next verse:

> Jesus answered and said to him, "Blessed are you, Simon Bar-Jonah, for flesh and blood has not revealed this to you, but My Father who is in heaven."
> MATTHEW 16:17

CARNALITY BLOCKS IDENTITY

You cannot receive your true identity through mere carnality. The Bible says that the carnal mind is enmity against God, so your reasoning, your understanding, your education does not matter one bit. It doesn't matter if you went to Yale or Harvard or any other major university to get your degree. Your natural mind cannot comprehend the true identity of Christ. It must be revealed to you by His Spirit. It must be begotten in your spirit.

ID REQUIRED

This is why so many people can be under the presence of God but not understand or discern the presence of God. This is why so many people laugh and mock and cannot understand why you or I believe the things that we believe. Their carnal mind is a dividing wall between them and God. Their soul is warring with their spirit, and their spirit man is locked up so that they cannot comprehend.

Jesus said that flesh and blood had not revealed this truth to Peter. There was no way he could have grasped this in his mere carnality. Many of us try to identify the things of the Spirit through carnal ways. We measure the things of the Spirit with measuring cups of the flesh. And we miss out on what God is saying to us and where God is leading us because we try to add to the Spirit things that do not belong to the Spirit. But as soon as Peter identified Christ correctly, he received his Kingdom identity.

When a foreigner comes into this nation and wants to become a citizen of the United States, he has to go through a process to get a green card. In the same way, we must receive our heavenly citizenship. We need our ID card so we can receive access into those places that we can only reach through the Spirit of the living God. Have you been praying, "God, why can't I get through that door? God, why haven't I come into my destiny? God, why can't I reach what You have for me?" The truth is, you may be trying through the arm of the flesh! The Bible said that it's not by might or by power; it's by the Spirit of the Lord. We need to receive a holy green card! We need to receive our citizenship in the heavenly Kingdom. We need to learn to properly identify ourselves because we're not from this world!. We have a holy identity in heaven. We're citizens of a holy nation.

Peter could not receive his calling until he first under-stood his true identity. How will you learn your identity? Peter received it through the living Word, Jesus; in the same way, we receive it through God's holy Word. You may try to find it by having someone pray for you, someone blow on you, someone prophesy over you; but you will actually find it yourself if you get in the Word. If you'd open up the Bible, you'd find what God has for you. If you'd get in your prayer closet, He'd speak to you and you'd find your true calling. Don't keep waiting for someone else to come and help you. You and God can do it together!

If you ignore the Word and just try to operate in your flesh alone, you will forever wonder why you are not pros-pering. You will wonder why you don't have anything, aren't going anywhere, and aren't doing anything worthwhile! The next few verses revealed Peter's destiny:

> "And I also say to you that you are Peter, and on this rock I will build My church, and the gates of hell shall not prevail against it. And I will give you the keys of the kingdom of heaven, and whatever you bind on earth will be bound in heaven, and whatever you loose on earth will be loosed in heaven."
> MATTHEW 16:18–19

GATES CAN'T STOP US!

In Scripture, and in life, gates are meant to keep things out. But when we find our true identity, no gate can keep us from entering and spoiling the enemy's camp. You may be worried about the gates of hell, but the "gates" are not offensive—they are not going to hurt you. Gates are defensive—we are going to hurt them, when we know our true identity in Christ! When Peter received the revelation of who Jesus is and who he was in Him, the gates of hell could not prevail against him.

You're unstoppable when you realize your identity in Christ.

Do you need money? No gate can keep you from receiving the provision you need. Do you need favor? No gate can stop you from receiving the favor of the Lord. Do you need healing? No gate can keep you from receiving the healing that Jesus paid for on the cross. No gate can stop someone who receives their proper identity in Christ.

You're unstoppable when you realize your identity in Christ. No debt can stop you, no sickness or disease can stop you, no lying, wagging tongue can stop you, no accusations from hell can stop you. God will see you through when you are properly identified with Him.

It's one thing to receive Jesus into your heart, but it's another thing when you identify Him in your life as the Son of the living God...because you've moved from receiving a Savior into receiving the Son. When you receive the Son, then you come into sonship. In verse 19, Jesus said, *"And I will give you the keys of the kingdom."* Those are the access codes you need to receive heaven's blessings! Who was Jesus giving them to? He was talking to Peter—not to any of the other eleven disciples. He was talking exclusively to someone who had just properly identified Him and received his own identity in Him. He said, "YOU, Peter, I'm giving the keys to YOU. YOU have access granted. YOU have the ID required to get you through the doors that you need to pass through. I am giving to YOU the keys of the Kingdom of heaven, and whatever you bind on earth shall be bound in heaven, and whatever you loose on earth shall be loosed in heaven!"

Do you want to see some things loosed in your life? Are the things of God being held up for you? Are there blessings and promises that are still waiting to be fulfilled? They will come to pass when you receive your true identity.

HEAVEN'S STANDARDS OR THE WORLD'S STANDARDS?

It's funny that Jesus would do things completely different from the world of His day. In Jesus' time, the Pharisees and the Sadducees had created all sorts of different rules that the people had to obey before they could even begin to be in right standing with God. If Jesus had done things the way the religious rulers of His day wanted them done, no one could have been considered worthy to receive any blessings at all. But thank God, Jesus operates on a completely different system.

If we did things by our standards today, we would say to different people, "you're an apostle," "you're a prophet," "you're a teacher," "you're an evangelist," "you're a pastor," and on and on, based solely upon seeing natural results that were being brought forth in that person's life. But that's how the Pharisees judge. Some say, "I give the big offering; I deserve a front-row seat. I prophesy the loudest, so I must be a prophet." But you know, even a donkey can prophesy—that actually happened in the Old Testament. The fact that God was able to use you one time does not make you a prophet. When we are judging in the natural, some people may seem to be prophets who actually aren't prophets at all! Although natural results are necessary, we must be careful not to identify things only by the external appearance.

That's why Jesus has a problem with religious people, people who lack a true relationship with Him. Have you ever noticed the language Jesus uses to refer to the religious? "You bunch of snakes, vipers, hypocrites." That's how Jesus addressed the religious people of His day. If He were speaking today, would He be referring to you? Do you look only to the natural results to determine whether or not God is involved, or do you seek to find your true identity in Christ, and simply let the results follow? Now we don't need to trample on grace to excuse character flaws; character and integrity are necessary traits we need to convey Christ in every thing we do!

Although natural results are necessary, we must be careful not to identify things only by the external appearance.

Peter didn't have to do anything to qualify for Jesus' calling—except realize Jesus' identity and then apply it to himself: *"You are the Christ, the Son of the living God,"* he declared. Jesus called Peter out when he was a blundering, cursing fisherman, and gave him the keys to His Kingdom.

Some of us think we've got it all figured out. We are so holy; we read the Bible; we've been to Bible school; we've been prophesied over, and someone famous has blown on our foreheads. We've got it all figured out. But when I read the Bible, I see Jesus calling things that are not as though they were. I see Jesus looking at an unstable, blundering, cursing fisherman, a reed shaken in the wind, and when He approached this fisherman for the first time, He said,

"What's your name?" When the **fisherman** replied, "Simon Bar-Jona," Jesus said, "No more. **Your name is Peter**." That was their first introduction. Simon Bar-Jona's identity was immediately changed!

Wouldn't that blow your mind if that happened to you? What if you came up to me today, and I shook your hand as you told me your name. But then I said, "Lyle (or whatever your name is), good to meet you. But your name is not Lyle anymore. Your name is Phil." Would that not get your attention? Who am I to rename you Phil when I first meet you? But that's what happened when Peter first met Jesus Christ. His entire identity was changed.

Now, in Bible times names meant more than they do today. Names were a greater source of identification in that time. In American society, we may just name our kids after their parents or grandparents or aunts or uncles. We don't always think about the meanings of the names. But in the Bible they prayed about things, and children were named according to what God said about that child.

Even still, Jesus had to change Simon's name to Peter, the name that would reflect his destiny. Jesus chose a man to lead His Church who was quite rough around the edges. He was a person who, if you got in his face, he'd get back in yours! He had no qualms with finishing a fight. Jesus had to clean up Peter's mess every time he said or did something. If you remember, Peter was the one who cut off the ear of a soldier who had come to arrest Jesus in the Garden of Gethsemane—Jesus had to pick up that ear up from the ground and put it back on the soldier. Peter had a temper! He was completely emotional—ruled by his flesh. But at

Jesus' first meeting with him, the Savior said, "You're a rock. You're not emotional. You're not unstable. You're not erratic. You're a rock!" Jesus was calling those things that were not as though they were.

GOD LOOKS ON THE HEART!

W hen others see a shepherd boy, God sees a king. When man looks on the outward appearance, God looks on the heart. God changes our hearts and our natures—and our identity—so that we can fulfill the destiny He has for us. Jesus changed Simon's name to Peter, and He had a disciple for life.

One day Jesus took Peter and the other disciples to the top of a mountain, the Mount of Transfiguration. Before they knew it, both Elijah and Moses appeared before them all. Elijah, Moses, and Jesus were all there together, glowing with the glory of God. Can you imagine Peter's reaction? He literally fell down to the ground, overcome by the *Shekinah* glory of the Lord. When he finally came to himself, he said, "Jesus, I've got a fantastic idea! Let me build a tabernacle for all three of you!"

Sometimes Peter was too impetuous for his own good! I like to say "he was one French fry short of a Happy Meal." Or, sometimes it seemed like "the elevator didn't go all the way to the top floor!" He had some crazy ideas at times, but

Jesus still said that he was a rock—the rock on which He would build His Church. In the natural, we would never have called him a rock; we would have said he was unstable, too emotional, unable to get his act together. But Jesus looked beyond all of those faults and weaknesses of Peter and saw the root of what he would become.

Many people would have never recognized or received Abraham but would have kept on calling Abram. But God identified him as Abraham. Human beings would have looked for his children to validate that he was the father of many nations. But Christ saw his children before they were ever conceived. We would have looked at Sarai in the natural, and we would have said, "You're not a mother of nations. You can't even have children!" But God the Father called her, "Sarah." He identified her as a mother of nations, and then she became—guess what?—the mother of nations!

YOU ARE WHAT YOU ARE—BEFORE!

D id you know that it's possible to be an apostle and never have established a church? It's possible to be a prophet and never have prophesied a word? It's possible—according to the Bible. If you take it for what it says, anything is possible in your life—if God has destined it, it will take place!

"Before I formed you in the womb I knew you; before you were born I sanctified you; I ordained you a prophet to the nations."
JEREMIAH 1:5

Proper identity brings forth maximum productivity!

Notice it says, BEFORE! Before Jeremiah was ever conceived, God had big plans for him. Before Jeremiah had ever prophesied a word, he was ordained to be a prophet. That was the destiny that awaited him—and nothing could stop it! Before the proof of the prophet was revealed, Jeremiah was identified. In other words, proper identity brings forth maximum productivity!

GRACE VERSUS WORKS

We cannot pass off worldly accomplishments—buildings, land, television ministry, programs, books, or Christian media—as the validation of God's calling upon someone's life! Although many of these things are very helpful, they can never take the place of His grace. I've attended conferences and gatherings where people are accepted as apostles just because they have thousands of members in their churches or because they wrote a book or own a publishing company. If we are not careful, we can allow politics to pollute our judgment. We will say that someone is an apostle simply because they built a successful business or because they are on the "A" list of "Charismania"! This unholy mixture is trying to water down the apostolic movement in America and is trying to cause much confusion within the Body of Christ. As you mature, it is necessary to bear the fruit of your calling; however, we must be careful how we determine fruitfulness. For the greatest part of Christ's ministry, He had twelve members who attended His church, and He didn't have a mega-church building to put them in! John the Baptist spent most of his ministry in the middle of what many would call "nowhere." Still Christ said there was "no greater prophet than John"! The Apostle Paul spent over two years in Ephesus training twelve men (see Acts 19:1-10). Most people would have considered Paul to be a nobody with only a handful of disciples if they had caught him in the middle of this two-year timeframe. However, if you looked at these same twelve men just a little while later, you would find that they were responsible for all of Asia Minor hearing the Word of the Lord (see Acts 19:10)! Not to mention all the special miracles that came forth through Apostle Paul's ministry.

I could simply list the following references however I feel it's important to put them in print so you can read them again. These passages are evidence of the importance of not falling into the worldly trap of mistaking works and accomplishments with God's grace:

> Who has saved us and called us with a holy calling, not according to our works, but according to His own purpose and grace which was given to us in Christ Jesus before time began.
>
> 2 TIMOTHY 1:9

And if by grace, then it is no longer of works;
otherwise grace is no longer grace. But if it is
of works, it is no longer grace; otherwise work
is no longer work.

ROMANS 11:6

Through Him we have received grace and
apostleship for obedience to the faith among
all nations for His name.

ROMANS 1:5

Having then gifts differing according to the
grace that is given to us, whether prophecy,
[let us prophesy] according to the proportion
of faith.

ROMANS 12:6

According to the grace of God which is given
unto me, as a wise masterbuilder, I have laid
the foundation, and another buildeth thereon.
But let every man take heed how he buildeth
thereupon.

1 CORINTHIANS 3:10

But by the grace of God I am what I am, and
His grace toward me was not in vain; but I
labored more abundantly than they all, yet not
I, but the grace of God which was with me.

1 CORINTHIANS 15:10

For our boasting is this: the testimony of our
conscience that we conducted ourselves in the
world in simplicity and godly sincerity, not with
fleshly wisdom but by the grace of God, and
more abundantly toward you.

2 CORINTHIANS 1:12

But when it pleased God, who separated me from my mother's womb and called me through His grace.

GALATIANS 1:15

Of which I became a minister according to the gift of the grace of God given to me by the effective working of His power. To me, who am less than the least of all the saints, this grace was given, that I should preach among the Gentiles the unsearchable riches of Christ.

EPHESIANS 3:7–8

CALLED, CHOSEN, AND IDENTIFIED!

Let's take a look at a different passage in the New Testament that establishes this truth:

And when it was day, He **called** His disciples to Himself; and from them He **chose** twelve whom He also **named** apostles.

LUKE 6:13, EMPHASIS MINE

What does the Scripture say that Jesus called them? He called His twelve disciples. But who did He *name* them to be? Apostles! To repeat: Jesus didn't *call* these twelve men to be apostles; He *named* them apostles. When I looked up these words, I discovered an important difference between them.

Called = "summoned to oneself."
Chosen = "to pick out or choose for oneself."
Named = "commissioned; to give a name to; to name;
to endow."

In other words, Jesus gave these twelve men a new name, a new ID—a new identity in Him so that they could receive all that He had for them and so that they could become all that He had destined them to become.

In the same way, God has called you and named you as His own. He has given you a new identity so that you could be endowed with what you need to fulfill your destiny. Why do you need to be "identified" if you're already experiencing blessings? Sometimes that can happen, but in the true order of the spiritual realm, you identify something *first*, and then it begins to function in the way it was called to function. For example, in the beginning God said, "Let there be light." He called the light day. And from that day forward, it was day. It happened in that very same way throughout creation: God created something, then He named it, and it was able to fulfill its function. The moon was created, and there was night. The animals were created, then they were named and they were released to fulfill their various functions in the earth.

God wants to do the same thing in your life. He wants to bring you into the maturity and the fullness of your calling. You will fulfill your destiny when you walk in your identity with maturity!

That is what happened in my own life. If you had met me back in 1987, you would never have believed that God had called me to be an apostle. You would never have been able to identify my calling in the natural realm. In fact, you probably would have said there was no way that I had a godly purpose to fulfill! You wouldn't have seen an apostle of God—you would have just seen a lanky teenager, a skinny beanpole of a kid who was ignorant of the things of God. Even if you had seen me in 1992, you would have still argued with calling me an apostle. But thank God that He does not look at us the way that other human beings look at us! No one can discredit my ministry today. People might talk about me, but the fruit of my ministry demonstrates the calling that the Lord has placed upon my life.

I once prophesied to a woman whom the Lord said was called to be a prophet. But when I first met her you wouldn't have known that in the natural. She had never prophesied. She'd never sung a song of the Lord. But I prophesied over her that she would one day write the songs of the Lord, songs that would go out to the nations. She had never written a song before in her life! I also told her she would have a husband. At that time, she had no husband—and no prospect of one. There was no man in her life, and no engagement ring on her finger. But I could see in the realm of the Spirit the destiny that God had for her. Today she is married and has written music that has impacted nations.

When you find the identity that God has specifically for you and identify it by the Spirit of God, you will activate your calling. This will produce a release of your destiny into the world. That is what happened in Luke 6 when Jesus "named" the twelve men apostles. He identified them with the destiny He had for them.

CALLED VERSUS CHOSEN!

As I said before, first He called them. He "summoned them to Himself." The Bible says that many are called but few are chosen. The difference between being chosen and being called is that when the Lord calls you, He summons you to Himself, but when you are chosen, He has handpicked you for a very specific purpose. Then, when you are "named," you are released into your destiny. You are identified and commissioned to see His fruit come forth!

The Lord has instructed ministry gifts to raise up believers into their callings. However, if we're not careful, we can easily forget the destiny that He has for us. We need have to have all of the gifts and all of the callings operating within the Church in order to reach this world for Jesus Christ. We need *you* and the destiny that God has placed inside of you! We need apostles, prophets, teachers, evangelists, pastors—in the plural. The Church needs more than one of each of these! Every time you see an apostle mentioned in the Scriptures, you see more than one. The book of Acts talks about the apostles and the elders, but the apostles and the elders had to be identified within the Church before they could begin to serve their functions. Each of us needs to be identified in our calling so that we can fulfill everything God has for our lives.

Lost ID, False ID, and a Valid ID

Have you ever lost your wallet? What a horrible experience—to lose the very thing that contains your ID, your driver's license, your money, your credit cards, and even your photos! That is what happens when a person loses their identity—he or she loses so much more than their ID. Money is lost! Credit is lost! Memories are lost—and so much more.

Over the years it has become more and more common for students to produce false or fake ID cards. They generally do so with the intent to get into an establishment or buy something where it's required by law to card people prior to granting access or approving a purchase. All too often our young people are brought into contact with places or things that are intended for adults, long before they are mature enough to handle them. So it is in the Spirit when someone refuses to wait for the maturity of their identity.

Over the years, I have come across quite a few leaders in the Body of Christ who are trying to operate "vehicles" (i.e., their ministries) with invalid IDs. Many are trying to function today with yesterday's ID. I want to ask them, "What is God saying *today*, as opposed to what He said in 1982?" Too many of God's leaders are relying on outdated, obsolete spiritual technology. These ministers have become irrelevant; they are throwing water up in the air from yesterday's revivals singing, "It's beginning to rain, rain, rain! Hear the voice of the Father!" If only they would stop and listen to their own songs sometime. We must hear the voice of the Father! Man shall not live by bread alone, but by every word that proceeds out of the mouth of God!

We need a fresh, proceeding word from the Lord. I'm thankful for what God said to me in 1987, and I value every word He has spoken to me, but I must hear His voice today. I must stay current! The only way to stay "current" is by staying in the "current" of God's river. I must maintain a valid ID. This requires for me to go through the necessary updated training, prescribed processes, and examinations on a regular basis. Leaders, especially, need to do this! Too many leaders refuse to leave the road of ministry for a short period of time and listen to someone other than themselves. I've been around ministers who brag about their busy schedules; they say things like, "I'm never home to attend church; I'm always out preaching." No wonder they are still preaching the same messages that they were preaching ten to twenty years ago!

The only way to stay "current" is by staying in the "current" of God's river.

I have found out the hard way that I must take time to be refueled. Over the past few years, I have made it a habit to sit down for several weeks in my own church and have the elders teach, preach, and prophesy. This does several things. First, it gives me time to be refreshed and refueled. Second, it blesses the church to hear from all of the fivefold gifts. Third, it instills confidence in the leadership and the people, letting them know that I believe enough in them to sit under their ministry. I also try to get away and attend at least one or two conferences, aside from the ones I'm speaking in, so that I can focus on receiving the Word myself. I also pray, study God's Word, read books that encourage my spirit, as well as keep messages and worship songs on my iPod to listen to as I travel.

You may say, "Well, what about me? I'm not a leader." It's just as important for you to maintain a valid ID so that you can minister to those in your sphere of influence! Your family, your neighbors, and your coworkers need more than just your same old stale leftovers! They need you to minister out of fresh relationship and anointing! So, if your ID has lapsed, go in for an appointment with God today and get it updated. He's waiting to validate your ID. You never know, He just might reveal something new to you that will reveal amazing new blessings for your life!

ID THEFT

While on a ministry trip to Canada, I received a *USA Today* paper delivered to my room. The front page was titled, "ID Theft Costs Victims Businesses." Here is what it said: "About 27.3 million people have been victims of identity theft in the past five years—9.9 million victims in 2002 alone. There have been forty-eight billion dollars of losses to financial institutions and businesses, and five billion dollars made up the out-of-pocket expenses for the victims."

Did you know that things that take place in the natural mimic what takes place in the spiritual realm? There was a member of our church who was a victim of identity theft—in the natural realm—recently. Someone stole his credit-card number and was using it to charge up purchases in various places. They stole his identity and took his money! Just as that happens in the natural realm more often, it also happens in the supernatural realm. You may have experienced it yourself: the glory of God, His anointing, His power, His miracle signs and wonders, and the financial provision He has stored up for you! But maybe you have experienced all of that being taken from you *illegally* because the enemy has tried to steal your identity!

Take a look at the devil's usual *modus operandi*, as outlined in this familiar verse of Scripture. Jesus Himself said:

> "The thief does not come except to steal, and to kill, and to destroy. I have come that they may have life, and that they may have it more abundantly."
>
> JOHN 10:10

Stealing, killing, and destroying—that is what our enemy does best. And identity theft is one of the greatest tools the devil has been using to try to keep you from fulfilling your destiny in God. But the devil is a liar!

> …for he (the devil) is a liar and the father of it.
>
> JOHN 8:44

WANTED: IDENTITY THIEVES

As we have just seen, *"the thief comes only to steal and kill and destroy"* (John 10:10a). There are twenty-four tactics the devil uses to steal our identities from us, what I like to call "identity thieves." But you can stop each of these thieves in their tracks by speaking the Word of God and refusing to allow them to gain a foothold in your life.

1. **Fear:** Isaiah 41:10, 13; 43:1; 54:4, 14; 2 Timothy 1:7; Hebrews 13:6; 1 John 4:18

2. **Doubt and Unbelief:** Matthew 13:58; 17:20; 21:21; Mark 6:6; 11:23, 24; Romans 4:20; Hebrews 3:12, 19; 4:6, 11

3. **Deception and Manipulation:** 1 Corinthians 15:33; Luke 21:8; Ephesians 4:14; Galatians 3:1; 2 Thessalonians 2:3

4. **Familiarity:** Matthew 13:53–58; 16:21–24; Numbers 12:1–10, 13–16; 16:1–4, 8–10; John 1:10–11

5. **Murmuring and Complaining:** Psalm 144:14; John 6:43; Philippians 2:14; 1 Corinthians 10:10; Matthew 25:26; Romans 12:11

6. **Slothfulness:** Ecclesiastes 10:18; Proverbs 12:24, 27; 19:15; Romans 12:11

7. **Wrong Relationships:** Deuteronomy 22:10; Proverbs 13:20; 22:24–25; 1 Corinthians 15:33; 2 Corinthians 6:14

8. **Traditions of Men:** Matthew 15:2–3, 6; Mark 7:1

9. **"Stinking Thinking":** Romans 12:1–2; Philippians 4:8–9; James 1:1–2

10. **Gossip, Accusations, and Slander ("G.A.S."):** Psalm 31:13; Romans 8:33–39; Revelation 12:10; 1 Timothy 5:1

11. **Greed and Materialism:** Luke 6:11, 13; Acts 8:18, 20; 1 Peter 5:2; 1 Timothy 3:8; 6:10

12. **Unforgiveness:** Matthew 6:12–15; Mark 11:25–26; Luke 23:24; 1 John 1:9

13. **Breaking Covenant:** Romans 1:31; 2 Timothy 3:1–5

14. **Robbing God:** Malachi 3:8–12; Acts 5:1–10

15. **Rebellion:** Numbers 16:1–3, 12–14; 1 Samuel 15:23; Isaiah 1:19, 20

16. **Politics ("Men Pleasing"):** Colossians 3:22; Acts 4:18–20

17. **Poverty and Debt:** Proverbs 10:15; 28:22

18. **Generational Curses:** Exodus 20:5; Deuteronomy 5:9

19. **Lack of Discernment:** 1 Kings 3:9; Ezekiel 44:23; Malachi 3:18; Luke 12:56; Hebrews 5:14; 1 Chronicles 12:32

20. **Immaturity and Impatience:** 1 Corinthians 13:11; Galatians 4:1–2; Numbers 20:11, 12; Hebrews 6:12; 10:36; 12:1; James 1:3, 4

21. **Bitterness and Offense ("B.O."):** Matthew 11:6; 13:57; Mark 4:7; Luke 17:1; Psalm 119:165

22. **Pride:** Philippians 2:5–9; Proverbs 16:18; 29:23; James 4:6; 1 Peter 5:5

23. **Sexual Sin:** Genesis 34:1–3; Hebrews 13:4; 1 Corinthians 6:15–18

24. **Negative Confession ("Watch Your Mouth"):** Proverbs 12:18; -18:21; 21:23; James 3:5–=6

HOW TO PREVENT ID THEFT

Although ID theft is very costly and destructive, the good news is that it is preventable! In the natural, there are seven steps to follow to prevent identity theft. From these, I have derived seven steps to prevent *spiritual identity theft.*

1. Don't give out your social security number. The most important item to an identity thief is your social security number.

   In the spiritual realm, this reveals a very important principle: Be careful to whom you reveal your identity! Not everyone will be happy when you discover who you really are. Remember Joseph? When he shared his spiritual identity with his brothers, they became very upset and threw him in a pit (see Genesis 37:5).

2. Check your credit report regularly. By checking regularly, you will notice any unusual discrepancies before they become a major problem.

   In the spiritual realm, check in with heaven on a regular basis. As Smith Wigglesworth once said, "It's not how long you pray, it's how long you go without praying." Make sure you stay close to God in prayer, and He will help you become aware of any problems before they become too big for you to handle.

3. Monitor your credit-card bills for charges that you haven't made. This is the best way to tell if someone else is charging on your card.

   You must also stay alert and awake in the Spirit so that the enemy cannot slip in and steal your identity. You must be sober and vigilant (see 1 Peter 5:8)! I like the way the Message Bible puts it:

   Keep a cool head. Stay alert. The Devil is poised to pounce, and would like nothing better than to catch you napping!

4. Buy a shredder and shred all papers before tossing them into the trash. It's awfully hard to use information that has been shredded.

   Even in the spiritual realm, you must shred, shred, shred! You must shred anything that the enemy could use to hurt you! Don't allow anything harmful from your past to remain in your life. Put it in the shredder of Jesus' blood, the shredder of His Word, the shredder of His name and His Spirit. When you confess your sins, you are putting them through the shredder. Declare God's Word over your past, and dance on the devil's head! When you declare the victory and dance in confidence, you are shredding the darkness of your past and opening up a brighter future!

5. Don't give your credit-card numbers to strangers. No matter how trustworthy a person might seem, they could be waiting to assume your identity.

   It is a sad fact that not everyone is who they seem to be. Sometimes people actually try to get close to you so they can steal from you. Leaders, especially, must walk in a higher level of discernment in these days, because there are many ID thieves who would prefer to steal another man's work than to pay the price and birth their own. Leader, make sure that you know those who labor among you. Spend time with them. Test them. Listen to the prophets and leaders whom you have already proven before giving out any important information.

6. Don't give personal information over the phone unless you initiated the call. Even if you initiate the call, be sure you know that the recipient of your personal information is valid.

Spiritually, you must also know a person's identity before you share your own identity with them. This is primarily the case when you are sharing important matters with someone else. I have learned the hard way that such revelation should generally be reserved for intimate relationships and not mere acquaintances.

7. Guard your identity as you would any other valuable asset. Your identity in someone else's hands can ruin you and your credit.

Guard your spiritual identity! Just as you would never knowingly give out important information that would allow someone to steal from you, you must also be proactive and guard the spiritual identity that God has given you. Don't give out information to religious Pharisees and Sadducees. They will only use it against you!

YOU DON'T HAVE TO PUT UP WITH IT!

The devil has been a liar and a murderer from the very beginning of time, and he continues to practice his deceit and destruction to this day. The good news is that you don't have to put up with it! The devil can and must be defeated in your life. You *must* know who you are in Christ!

You must know who Christ is and what your calling is! And you must be determined to fulfill the purpose for which you were placed on this earth.

He will identify you with His hand—through His apostles, His prophets, His evangelists, and His pastors and teachers.

It is the enemy's mission to keep you from learning your true identity. He wants to keep you from your destiny. But John 10:10 boasts of hope for you! Just look what Jesus came and did for you. He said, "I have come that you might have life and that you might have it more abundantly." Would you like to have a more abundant life? God wants to give that to you—and you can receive it when you properly identify yourself with Christ and allow Him to properly identify you.

He will identify you with His hand—through His apostles, His prophets, His evangelists, and His pastors and teachers. They have been graced with the ability to help identify who you are. And when you receive that identity, you will be able to begin to fulfill your destiny.

THE FATHER'S AFFIRMATION BRINGS FORTH IDENTITY

In 1 Corinthians 4, we learn of the power of the Father's affirmation and the blessing of sonship.

> For though you might have ten thousand instructors in Christ, yet you do not have many fathers; for in Christ Jesus I have begotten you through the gospel.
> 1 CORINTHIANS 4:15

Most people think of those words *"begotten you through the gospel"* as referring only to people getting saved. But I would like to take it further and say that it also refers to becoming a son. It's one thing to give birth to children, but it's an entirely different thing to shape a son. It's not that hard to bring someone into the Kingdom of God and see them saved. We can fill ball stadiums up and let an evangelist preach, and you'll see many people saved, but that does not take the place of the "father anointing" that's needed to bring them into their true identity.

> For though you might have ten thousand instructors in Christ, yet you do not have many fathers; for in Christ Jesus I have begotten you through the gospel. Therefore I urge you, imitate me. For this reason I have sent Timothy

to you, who is my beloved and faithful son in
the Lord, who will remind you of my ways in
Christ, as I teach everywhere in every church.
1 Corinthians 4:15–17

We can see in this passage of Scripture that fathers "be-get" sons, and sons remind us of that father's heart and anointing. Have you ever heard it said, "He looks just like his daddy"? Now that's a compliment! Our society today places so much emphasis on "being yourself" that we often forget that we do not belong to ourselves alone. Paul said, "Be an imitator of me!" He said, "Follow me as I follow Christ!" Paul wanted everyone to know the good things God had given him through Jesus, and he wanted everyone to experience it with him. He wanted to pass those things on as a father would pass on an inheritance to his son.

The same thing took place in the lives of the Old Testament prophets Elijah and Elisha. God had put something in Elijah that Elisha needed to receive. Elisha could only receive his identity as he emulated his spiritual father. Elisha eventually came into his own ministry. Elisha did receive the double portion and fulfilled his own unique purpose. But there was a season when every step he took looked just like his daddy's. There was a season when every time he got up to prophesy, he sounded just like his daddy. The voice was the same, the words were the same—he was emulating his spiritual father, and through that obedience, his ministry was built.

Even today I can still hear my own dad's voice in my own. I'll say something sometimes, and it is as if my dad's walked right into the room. The older I get, it seems, the more I sound like him. Have you ever experienced that?

You say something or do something and you suddenly real-ize, *That's just like my mom!* Or, *Oh, that's just like my dad!* Have you ever been around someone for a length of time, and you find that after awhile you are completing the other person's sentences? That's the way Elisha was with Elijah. When Elijah was taken away to heaven in the chariot of fire, Elisha did not say, "My teacher, my teacher!" He cried out, "My father, my father!" even though Elijah was not his natural father. But that fatherly anointing was on Elijah's life to impart the anointing to his spiritual son, Elisha.

The identity we must have to access God's blessings for us will largely be found in our ability to be a son or a daughter.

The identity we must have to access God's blessings for us will largely be found in our ability to be a son or a daugh-ter—to be a follower of a father.

There has never been a generation like the generation we're raising right now. The prophets and the apostles that have walked this earth in years past will pale in comparison to our sons and to your daughters—both our natural chil-dren and our spiritual ones. The Word says, "Your sons and your daughters will prophesy. They will have dreams. They will have visions and they will go to the nations" (see Joel 2:28). As a child I did not know my calling or have any idea of my purpose in life. But *my* son did. I knew two years before my son was born what he would look like. I saw my child come into the kitchen in front of me, and I knew his name. The Lord had told me, "His name will be Hunter. I've called your son to be a hunter, and he'll protect my people.

Angels will visit him as he stands on the platform, and he will prophesy of things to come. Your son will speak to presidents, to the rulers of the world."

Two years before my son was born, I was faithful to write those words from the Lord down on a piece of paper. When Hunter was in his mother's womb, I would get up to her belly and I would speak to him: "You mighty man of God, you're a prophet to the nations. Kings will listen to your voice. Presidents will receive you. You will speak with great specificity. Accuracy is your portion, son." That is what I prophesied while he was still in the womb. When he came out, I'd hold him, and I'd walk the floors and pray, speaking over him, "You're a prophet to the nations." And when he was eighteen months old, I'd stand him up on the pulpit and I would say, "Son, what are you?" He'd tell me, "A mighty man of God and a prophet!" He knew what his destiny was because his father had revealed it to him!

So many people today can't figure out who they are, what they're doing, where they're going. They don't know their own identity! And so much of our identity is wrapped up in what our earthly fathers, and our heavenly Father, impart to us. God has given me a fathering anointing to affirm your calling in the Lord and to begin to identify who you are for the Kingdom. Other people may have called you things that you're not. Other people may have limited you by giving you the wrong name. But I affirm to you that you are called of God to do great things for His Kingdom and His people in this hour.

THE WIFE'S IDENTITY

It is not only important to find out your identity as an individual, but those who are married must begin to find their identity in their marriage partnership before the Lord. The marriage covenant was established by God in the very first book of the Bible, the book of Genesis, the book of beginnings. God created the world first, then filled the world with animals, birds, fish, and other creatures. He then created Adam from the dust of the earth and breathed His life into this man, making him a living soul. God brought all of the animals before Adam to be *named*, or *identified*, however, you will notice in Genesis 2:20, *"there was not found a help meet for him."* God knew that it was not good for the man to be alone, so He took action:

> And the LORD God caused a deep sleep to fall on Adam, and he slept; and He took one of his ribs, and closed up the flesh in its place. Then the rib which the LORD God had taken from man He made into a woman, and He brought her to the man. And Adam said: "This is now bone of my bones, and flesh of my flesh; she shall be called Woman, because she was taken out of Man." Therefore a man shall leave his father and mother and be joined to his wife, and they shall become one flesh. And they were both naked, the man and his wife, and were not ashamed.
>
> GENESIS 2:21–25

Who named the wife? *Adam* called his wife's name "Eve." There is an important scriptural principle to be found here: Who brings identity to the wife? Who calls his wife's name? God assigned that task to the husband of the wife.

On a personal note, my wife, Deborah Ashley, and I have walked through this process of identification. When my wife was born her parents named her Deborah Ashley. Her mom and dad took her for a follow-up doctor's visit, and one of the office staff said, "Oh, no, not another Debbie!" This upset her mother, and she changed her name to Ashley Karen!

Deborah has a rich godly heritage, a wealth of knowledge of Scripture, and a passionate relationship with Christ. She has always walked closely with the Lord, however over the years she experienced an internal struggle and resistance from operating in the fullness of her calling.

Beginning in 1995, she received the first of many prophetic words that God called her to be a Deborah to the Body of Christ! One day after receiving one of these confirming prophetic words, I pointed this out to my wife. She then shared with me the story of how her mother had changed her name from Deborah Ashley to Ashley Karen. She pulled out her original birth certificate and there it was— Deborah Ashley Brady! After much prayer, I shared with my wife that God revealed to me that God had given her parents the original name, Deborah Ashley, but the enemy had used that staff member in the doctor's office to try to steal her identity and destiny. She was in agreement, so one day, under the unction of the Holy Spirit, I prophetically declared that her name was Deborah Ashley and that she was called as a prophet to speak the Word of God into the lives of people. Now she is prophesying, singing, preaching, and teaching with a greater unction and anointing. Since she found her *identity*, timidity has been broken, and she ministers in a new level of freedom and *authority*.

You can find this same principle later on in Genesis. After God gave Abraham a new ID, He commissioned Abraham to properly identify Sarah. Abraham changed his wife's name!

> Then God said to Abraham, "As for Sarai your wife, you shall not call her name Sarai, but Sarah shall be her name. And I will bless her and also give you a son by her; then I will bless her, and she shall be a mother of nations; kings of peoples shall be from her."
> GENESIS 17:15–16

When a woman is married to a godly man, the husband will bring out of her, her true identity. He will bring out of that woman her destiny. Things that may have been locked up on the inside of her will be revealed to that husband in order that he may draw them out of her!

Ladies, you don't need women's lib—you need to help your husband to follow the Lord. If you affirm your husband, your husband will love you more than your wildest dreams, and you will become who you need to become in Christ. Your identity will not come from me—or from reading this book. Your identity will come from the most anointed man in your life—the one you go home with every night. You don't need me to pray for you—your husband can roll over in bed and pray for you! You don't need a prophet to speak over your life—you just need to affirm your husband enough to believe that God can speak to him and allow him to call forth your destiny in your life! Start calling out the greatness from inside of him, because what's in him is the ability to call forth what's inside of you.

There is an order to things. God created man, and then out of the man, He created the woman. Adam called his wife's name "Eve." The word *Eve* means "living" in the Hebrew. It means "life." So Adam, in essence, pronounced, "Woman, you are life to me! I find life in my wife. I find life in my help meet." Eve was not only alive herself, but she had the ability to produce life.

The greatest gift a man could ever receive is his wife. And how he treats that gift will determine how far he is able to go in his destiny.

Things have to be put in order in marriage. I know that for some people this is difficult to hear. Since the '60s, many women basically said that men were completely unnecessary to them. They believe that they can stand on their own. But after you read the next few pages, you'll find out that the opposite is actually true!

What about the single woman? The good news is that you're complete in Christ. Christ is your husband (see Isaiah 54:5). But when you meet the man that God has for you, he will hold keys to help unlock your destiny. God *gave* Eve to man. *Eve* was the *gift*. The woman is the gift to man, not the other way around! That means that the greatest gift a man could ever receive is his wife. And how he treats that gift will determine how far he is able to go in his destiny. The Bible says that if you cannot rule your own home, you don't have any business trying to take authority in God's house.

You should never try to preach to somebody when you can't minister to your own wife. A man is to love his wife as his own body (see Ephesians 5). That's in the Book! When you identify your wife and you bring her into the person she is called to be, then she will have the ability to be a true help meet to you and bring out of you things you never knew were on the inside of you! Many men call this "nagging," but women have the uncanny ability to see what's on the inside of you and they're calling it out. Rise up, man of God! Allow your wife to motivate you to greatness! When you have a holy woman, a woman who is in the Word, a woman who is on her knees, a woman who loves God, who has her priorities in order—if she is calling something out of you, you need to realize that she very well could be right! She is the help meet whom God brought alongside of you to pull the greatness right out of you!

Some men in the Church today are looking for someone else to give them counsel when their greatest counselor sleeps beside them every night!

When you look back to that word *help meet* in the original Hebrew, it actually means "revealer of the evil one." Some men in the Church today are looking for someone else to give them counsel when their greatest counselor sleeps beside them every night! The greatest wisdom they need is already right there in front of them because their wife has been given as a help meet to them. Sometimes we call it intuition, a woman's intuition. But it has nothing to do with that. It's a woman's God-given makeup—their spiritual DNA. God put it within our help meet the ability to reveal the evil one when he tries to enter your life. Your wife may say, "Don't hire that person now."

Or, "I don't think you should make that investment." God put her beside you to reveal the evil one, and you need to pay attention! Your wife is a protection for you.

Ladies, when you're a help meet, your purpose is to make sure no evil touches your husband or your children. Why on earth would you talk badly about your man behind his back? Why would you speak negative words about the husband God gave you? You're using your own tongue to smite the one who is a shepherd over your family. Instead, you need to reveal the evil one in your lives. God will show you where the enemy would want to attack your family, your finances, your marriage or you health. When He does, you submit it to the one whom God has called to be the head of your house.

Many of us miss out on our destiny because we are too busy doing our own thing. A wife is either dead weight or a help meet. Many women say, "Well, if he would just love me like he's supposed to love me, then I'd follow him." Maybe he would show more love to you if you would help complete him! Maybe his parents never encouraged him. Maybe every boss he had always talked bad about him. But perhaps if you would say to him, "I'm with you," and mean it, he would be complete enough to love you like he's been called to love you.

And men, you may be saying, "Well, I'll love my wife when she submits to me. When she starts doing what I tell her to do, that's when I'll start loving her." But Jesus loved the Church and died for the Church before the Church ever began to love Him. God wants you to complete, not compete. Do you ever wonder why your house is not advancing? Jesus said that a kingdom divided against itself cannot stand.

STOLEN SEED

Through the years America has seen an epidemic of divorce. This has been the plan of the enemy. The devil wants to steal your seed, your destiny. He loves to do it by stealing your identity, both as an individual and as a husband and wife. When Moses was born, there was a decree issued to take the seed. When Jesus was born, the same thing occurred: there was a decree issued to take the seed. Satan tries to smite the shepherd-husband and scatter the flock, the children. Satan tries to steal the husband's identity and authority. He wants to decapitate the headship of the house. It used to be that in secular society, one out of every two marriages ended in divorce. Sadly, today, those same statistics hold true in the Church. Satan wants to steal your seed.

Rebellion in the marriage produces rebellion in the children.

Your identity and that of your children are wrapped up in the completion of the identity of your marriage. If a husband and wife are torn apart, the children are torn apart in the process. Why are there so many youth in prison today? Why is there so much crime among young people—abortions, unwed mothers, suicides? It's a spirit. Rebellion in the marriage produces rebellion in the children.

Submission to Authority Releases Identity

Husbands, you cannot expect your wife to come under your authority if you don't come under authority yourself. You may want your wife to submit, but if you can't submit to the leadership of a local church, you may never see it happen. I fear for marriages within the Church today because men are neglecting spiritual authority in their lives. Men make decisions for their families, for their businesses, for the important things in their lives without receiving any counsel from the Church. The Bible says there's wisdom in the multitude of counsel. If you're a wise man, you won't try to do it on your own—you'll stop and ask for directions.

Your identity is found under authority. Once submitted to God's delegated authority the husband identifies the wife. Together they make each other complete, and they create and identify their children. The children grow up and know their destiny in the Lord; then they marry and identify their own children. That is what will create healthy families in the earth—both spiritually and naturally.

IDENTITY IS FOUND IN GOD'S FAMILY!

God sets the solitary in families!
PSALM 68:6

When my wife and I were returning on an international flight back into the United States, the flight attendants passed out cards to each of the passengers that we were to fill out to be able to reenter the country. On that card, you first stated your "given name," and then your "family name." Your family name is your last name—it tells who you're related to, the people you come from and are connected to, your clan—your *identity*. If you are Jewish, you probably have a Jewish family name. If you are Hispanic, you probably have a Hispanic name. Your name associates you with your tribe, your clan, your people. It is part of who you are. You are probably referred to by that name every day of your life—every form you fill out, every test you take, every possible way that you can be identified will call you by that name.

Do you understand the significance of your spiritual identity? It is just as important as your "family name"— your natural identity with your natural family members. When you come into the Kingdom of Jesus Christ, you become a child of the Most High God and a brother or a sister of Jesus Himself. You are brought into a family—the local church, the Body of Christ—and you begin to identify yourself with your heavenly Father, your spiritual father and spiritual family. When you become a part of the local church, you become a part of a family, and in this family, you will learn more about your heavenly Father and who He has called you to be. You see, the local church is your clan, your tribe, your family! You get your family name, or ID, from the local church. For instance, I am Joshua Fowler of the Tribe of Legacy—The Legacy Clan. Legacy is my family name. In other words, my last, or family, name is Legacy!

Loyalty to God's House—the local church— is essential to walk in the fullness of your identity!

Everywhere the family members of Legacy Life Church go, they take the love of Christ in the spirit and DNA of their family. So it is with you or anyone who belongs to a local church. We should stay in our spiritual family like we do our natural family! Loyalty to God's House—the local church—is essential to walk in the fullness of your identity! All too often many people with genuine conversions and callings live in a constant state of confusion and chaos because they hop from one local church to another. God is

When you are set in His house, you will radiate and shine with the brilliance of His glory!

looking for loyal disciples, those who will keep covenant with Him and His delegated authority. He wants to set you in a family of believers, a local church, like a fine diamond is set in a beautiful ring! Just as the many facets of a diamond cannot be seen until it is placed in its proper setting, so it is in each of our lives. When you are set in His house, you will radiate and shine with the brilliance of His glory! Once you are set— planted in God's house—you will live a fruitful and productive life that flourishes on every side!

> Those who are planted in the house of the LORD
> shall flourish in the courts of our God.
> PSALM 92:13

MINISTRY ID

I believe that when you find your identity, any reproach and shame that you may have experienced will be lifted off of your life. You come from the tribe of the Lord, from the Kingdom clan. You are God's chosen offspring. You are the seed of His house. But you must go even further than that. On that form I filled out for the customs department on the flight back into the United States, they not only asked for my "family name," but they also asked for my "title." What is your title in the Body of Christ? Are you a prophet? Are you a pastor? Are you a teacher? Do you have the gift of helps? Are you an apostle? Are you called to be an Aaron or a Hur, to hold up the arms of God's leaders? Who are you? Although it's not about titles and positions but serving, it is very important for you to know why you were given to the Body! You have a purpose. Every part in the Body is there for a reason. You are important, and God has given you gifts and talents that must be used for His glory in His Kingdom. If you are an apostle, rise up and be God's apostle without shame or fear of what man will say. Don't hide behind other identities anymore! If God said that you are an apostle, then don't say that you're a pastor, a missionary, or an evangelist. If God's called you to be His prophet, then don't say that you're a motivational speaker. Likewise, if God has called you to be a pastor or a businessman, then don't take on another identity to gain the approval of men. Be yourself! Be who God has called you to be, and you will be blessed. Walk in the ministry ID He has given you, and you will experience a greater level of His authority and favor than you ever have experienced before.

THE THIRD DAY— THE THIRD STEP: IDENTIFICATION

As we learned earlier from Luke 6:13, God has called, chosen, and named us, giving us a purpose for our lifetime on this earth. The Bible says that many are called, but few are chosen. God first calls you; He summons you to Himself. Then He chooses you; He moves you into your calling. Some of you have received His call. You may have been moving toward that calling. But you have yet to take the third step: identification. Each of us must be called, chosen, and identified by the Lord before we can truly fulfill His purposes.

The Bible refers to several things occurring in threes. The Trinity exemplifies this with the Father, the Son, and the Holy Spirit. It was on the third day that Jesus arose from the dead. He experienced three things: death, burial, and resurrection.

Right now I believe very strongly that we are in the Third Day of the Church. In 2000 we entered the third millennium—the Third Day—since Jesus Christ walked on the earth. The Bible says that a thousand years is a day and a day is as a thousand years to God (see 2 Peter 3:8).

On the First Day the Church was called forth by Christ. On the Second Day the Church was chosen to do the will of the Father. But now, in this Third Day, it is time for the Church's identification to come! It is time for the world to see why God has sent us out, why He has commissioned us to carry the Gospel of His Kingdom to the world. He could not reveal it in the outer court of the Temple, but He will reveal it beyond the veil, in a fresh and greater power and anointing.

This word is not just for the Church as a whole, but it is for you, specifically, as a believer in Jesus Christ. There is a third-day process in your life. Even as you read this book, you may be receiving the mantle to build a business, help finance the vision of a local church, or to become a prophet to the nations. You may be receiving an apostolic, prophetic, evangelistic, pastoral, or teaching mantle. You may not yet feel called to these things, but God will choose you for His specific purposes, and then He will brand that calling upon your heart and spirit. There is a necessary process that you must go through to see that calling fulfilled in your life. It takes perseverance and patience to see it through—to see your destiny fulfilled.

God will choose you for His specific purposes, and then He will brand that calling upon your heart and spirit.

Throughout the entire process, the most important thing is to remain close to the Lord. Even before you are summoned by Him, you must learn to lay your head on His shoulder and love Him, being willing to serve Him in whatever He would ask you to do. Only out of that ministry to Him comes the desire and passion to minister to others.

Once Jesus called His disciples, He identified them. He gave them the name "apostle," literally putting His name onto them. Sometimes I wonder what most people would think if this happened today. Jesus took people in from the fringes of society—He knew the people He was choosing were rough fishermen or hated tax collectors. But He chose them anyway. He took Peter and said, "I know you have been a fisherman all your life, but now you're an apostle." To Matthew, He said, "You've been a tax collector for years, but now you are My apostle, called to take My message of love and grace to the world." He didn't just chose people from humble or hated professions. He chose a doctor, Luke, to write one of the Gospels. It doesn't matter who you are, what training you have, or what you might have done before in your life—God is ready to call you out and bring you into a whole new season of destiny, a season of fulfillment of the plans that He has for you!

Never forget that Jesus calls things that are not as though they are. He called unstable Peter to become the rock on which He would build His Church. Near the end of Jesus' time on earth, He spoke to Peter and confirmed what his destiny would be. Jesus prophesied that Peter would be tempted by the enemy, but Jesus' calling was stronger in Peter's life than anything the devil could throw at him. Look closely at what Jesus said:

> And the Lord said, "Simon, Simon! Indeed, Satan has asked for you, that he may sift you as wheat. But I have prayed for you, that your faith should not fail; and when you have returned to Me, strengthen your brethren."
> LUKE 22:31–32

Isn't it wonderful to have Jesus pray for you? How effective do you imagine the prayers of the Lord are on your behalf? The Bible tells us that even now Jesus is seated at the right hand of the Father, interceding for us. Jesus knows everything that we face—the challenges that stand in our way that must be overcome before we can fulfill what He has for us. But Jesus looks at us and sees our great potential, and then He prays that we will overcome. Jesus saw a rock in Peter—even though He knew perfectly well that Peter would deny Him three times in one night.

> Then He said, "I tell you, Peter, the rooster shall not crow this day before you will deny three times that you know Me."
> LUKE 22:34

But still Jesus affirmed Peter's identity as a rock-solid believer! He was saying, you will return and when you do, strengthen your brothers. No matter what comes or goes, you will carry out the things I have called you to do—with stability and faithfulness!

As I stated earlier, the revelation Peter had of Jesus—that He was *"the Christ, the Son of the living God"*—qualified him to receive his true identity. Once he correctly identified Christ, Christ identified him. In the same way, your identity must be found *in Him.* There is no other way for you to find fulfillment in this life. The Word says that in Him we live and move and have our being (see Acts 17:28). When we pray in Jesus' name, we aren't just reciting a magical phrase that will make all of our prayers come true—we are coming to God clothed in the identity of His Son, Jesus Christ. When you stand before the Father, He sees His Son. The heavenly Father sees Jesus when He looks at you. Your identity is found in Him!

> "You did not choose Me, but I chose you and appointed you that you should go and bear fruit, and that your fruit should remain, that whatever you ask the Father in My name He may give you."
>
> JOHN 15:16

We can speak to devils in Jesus' name. We can speak to sickness and disease and poverty in the name of Jesus—with His authority and in His identity.

> "And these signs will follow those who believe: In My name they will cast out demons; they will speak with new tongues, they will take up

> serpents; and if they drink anything deadly, it
> will by no means hurt them; they will lay hands
> on the sick, and they will recover."
> MARK 16:17–18

We are in Christ, and Christ in us is the hope of glory! (see Colossians 1:27). We are in Him, and He is in us, and the devil can't see where we end and where He begins. The enemy just knows he'd better back off because we look just like our Daddy!

> "And these signs will follow those who believe:
> In My name they will cast out demons; they
> will speak with new tongues, they will take up
> serpents; and if they drink anything deadly, it
> will by no means hurt them; they will lay hands
> on the sick, and they will recover."
> MARK 16:17–18

IDENTITY PRAYER

Thank God for the anointing that destroys every yoke! (see Isaiah 10:27). It's not by chance that you are reading this book. God has commissioned me to come into agreement with you so that you will come into your identity and fulfill your destiny! I release the anointing into your life right now. I release the yoke-destroying, burden-removing anointing wherever you are, this very moment. I command any curse that has been spoken over you to be removed in the name of Jesus. I command those limiting words that have been spoken over your life to give up their power. If you have ever said that you would not be able to fulfill God's call, that you would not be able to achieve this, that you're not called and anointed of the Lord, or that you don't have enough education or you're not smart enough to succeed, I command those words right now to loose you and let you go in the name of Jesus. By the authority of the Word of God and in the name of Jesus, I release your true identity. As you begin to identify Christ Jesus as the Son of the living God, I declare that you will come under the hand of the Almighty God and that you will be properly identified through His apostles and His prophets and the other ministry gifts in His Church. I state boldly that you will be raised up—and the devil will not be able to stop you!

In the name of Jesus, I speak to those finances that have been stolen from you because of identity theft, and I command the enemy to give them back sevenfold. I speak to that marriage that's been shattered and destroyed, and by the authority of the Word of God, I command it to be properly identified as a godly marriage that glorifies the Lord. I speak to those children who have gone astray, that they would come home and receive their identity and begin to fulfill their destiny. I declare and decree this in Jesus' mighty name! Amen

IDENTITY CONFESSION

(Speak this confession out loud.)

I take authority over every limiting word, every curse that has been spoken, every thought that has come from the pit of hell, every word that was spoken by anyone that has limited what God desires to do in my life, and I renounce them in the name of Jesus! Those word curses must come off of me now in the name of Jesus. I take back anything that has been stolen because of ID theft. I come out from under any misidentification, and I receive my God-given identity. I shall walk in the blessings of the Lord from this day forward. I am who God says I am, and I can do everything He has called me to do. For whom God calls, He equips. I have been called and chosen, and I am walking into the fullness of my identity. Every day I am increasing in wisdom, stature, and favor with God and men. I lay hold of everything that God has for my life. I will be fruitful and multiply! I am blessed to be a blessing, and I will carry God's presence to everyone whom He sends me to. In Jesus' name, amen!

CONCLUSION

As you speak those words, I affirm to you that you are called, that you are chosen, and that God is identifying you. You will succeed, and you will prosper. You will reach the fullness of time for your destiny; you will see your *kairos* moment! There will be a release of divine favor on your behalf. There will be open doors in your life, which God has opened and that no man can shut. Opportunities will begin to come into your life that will be beyond what you could ever imagine. A release of favor, a release of supernatural increase, a release of supernatural abundance, and a release of the finances that have been stolen from you is about to take place. The enemy must repay! Traditions of men and religious systems that have held you back are rendered powerless. They are declared null and void!

Every check that the enemy has written with your old name on it is cancelled in the name of Jesus. It will not be able to find its way to you anymore, because that's not your name and you don't live at that spiritual address anymore!

Now, every check from God that has your new name, your true identity on it, will make there way to you! As you discover your true Identity in Christ, you will be equipped and empowered to do all that God has called you to do! You will come into the fulness of your time. God's plans for your life will come to maturity and you will possess the ID required to access the fulness of your destiny!

OTHER BOOKS AND RESOURCES
BY DR. JOSHUA FOWLER

Governors
of Praise

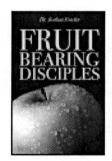

Fruit Bearing
Disciples

Legacy Life

Access Granted

You may order CD/DVD Teaching Series and
other resources at:
www.legacylife.org or 407-654-3344

CONTACT AND BOOKING INFORMATION

If you are interested in scheduling Dr. Fowler to
minister in your church, conference or gathering
you can contact the ministry at:
407-654-3344
or
info@legacylife.org

To order additional copies of
ID REQUIRED
have your credit card ready and call
1 800-917-BOOK (2665)

or e-mail
orders@selahbooks.com

or order online at
www.selahbooks.com

or online at
www.legacypress.us

Printed in the United States
123451LV00001B/127-312/A